The Archaeologist's Handbook

As well as being the author of the best-selling (and very silly) Eddie Dickens novels, Philip Ardagh has written numerous non-fiction works, including *Did Dinosaurs Snore?*, *Why Are Castles Castle-Shaped?* and *The Hieroglyphs Handbook*, the companion volume to *The Archaeologist's Handbook*. At the last count, his work has been translated into at least ten languages (11, if you count Latin) and he is a familiar speaker at festivals and events all over the UK and Ireland, including a number for the Young Friends of The British Museum. His passion for history and archaeology is matched only by the stupendous bushiness of his beard.

by the same author
published by Faber & Faber

Fiction

Books One and Two of the Eddie Dickens Trilogy
AWFUL END
DREADFUL ACTS

Unlikely Exploits 1:
THE FALL OF FERGAL

Non-fiction

THE HIEROGLYPHS HANDBOOK
Teach Yourself Ancient Egyptian

DID DINOSAURS SNORE?
100½ Questions About Dinosaurs Answered

WHY ARE CASTLES CASTLE-SHAPED?
100½ Tricky Questions About Castles Answered

THE
ARCHAEOLOGIST'S
HANDBOOK

PHILIP ARDAGH

Illustrated by Kevin Maddison

faber and faber

For Derek Colby of Swansea,
whose enthusiasm for the first handbook is not
forgotten and will always be much appreciated.

First published in 2002 by Faber and Faber Limited
3 Queen Square, London WC1N 3AU

Printed in Italy

A CIP record for this book
is available from the British Library

ISBN 0-571-20687-5

2 4 6 8 10 9 7 5 3 1

CONTENTS

'Archaeology is a lovely business...'

A FOREWORD FROM SANDI TOKSVIG
PRESIDENT OF THE YOUNG FRIENDS OF THE BRITISH MUSEUM

Archaeology, apart from being incredibly difficult to spell, is a lovely business. Where else can you mess about in the dirt looking as though the only things you've dug up recently are the clothes you're wearing? The truth is, though, archaeology is still an 'ology'. There are a few things that everyone from amateur to boffin ought to know, other than the fact that digging is best done downwards.

This marvellous handbook covers the lot. In here is everything you need to know; from where to start looking to what you do when you find something. It is packed with great information and none of it as dull and dry as an old bone in a fish kettle. (Although, actually, if you find one of those it'll probably be because you read this book.)

Finally: do be careful what you put in your rubbish today. It may well be the archaeology of tomorrow.

SANDI TOKSVIG

'The most exciting detective work there is...'

A MESSAGE FROM THE AUTHOR

Some people think of archaeology as the 'getting-your-hands-dirty' branch of history. In a sense that's true. Whereas history relies on the written word (prehistoric times being the time before writing), archaeology relies on the other physical evidence people left behind, from prehistoric times to the much more recent past.

When archaeologists talk about 'artefacts' they mean every kind of object from the most common, such as a cooking pot, to the rarest of the rare. These, and other excavated evidence – buildings, earthworks, old roads and even the bones of our ancestors (and the bones of what they ate) – are the main materials used by archaeologists to build up a picture of what us humans have been up to during our 100,000-or-so years on this planet. Archaeology is detective work; some of the most exciting detective work there is.

The Archaeologist's Handbook takes a look at the role of archaeologists from the discovery of an artefact or archaeological site to the identification, dating, preservation, restoration and understanding of what has been found. In it, we look at the most basic archaeological techniques to the latest technological advances used to assist the modern archaeologist. We look at the various branches of archaeology and how archaeologists with different skills and expertise work together, and with experts from other fields – including geologists, biologists and those all-important historians – to help create a better understanding of our ancestors, whatever part of the world they might have lived in.

I say 'we' because, although I wrote this book, I am indebted to all those experts – both professional and amateur – who made it possible for me to complete my most ambitious project to date: an easy-to-understand guide to one of the most fascinating and fantastic areas of exploration left to humankind; the study of what has gone before. My heartfelt thanks to them and, once again, to my editor Suzy Jenvey. I should stress, however, that – as always – any errors are mine.

I hope that this book helps to give a clear picture of the important and exciting role of archaeologists today and may even inspire you to become involved in a local archaeological group or society, at the very least!

PHILIP ARDAGH

Dig it!

WHY SO MUCH ARCHAEOLOGY IS BURIED

Something which always puzzled me when I was younger was why archaeologists had to dig to find things. It's not as if everyone used to live underground, so why are the remains of their buildings and possessions often found under metres of earth?

For safekeeping

The most startlingly obvious answer is because many finds – many artefacts – were originally buried in the first place. Treasure was buried for safekeeping, then lost or forgotten (or the owner died). There were no banks, building societies or safety deposit boxes, so the best place to keep something safe was in a filled-in hole in the ground – sometimes in a bag, pot or box – away from prying eyes. That's why people talk of finding 'a crock of gold'. A crock was a pot, as in crockery.

The people themselves

People themselves were buried, often with goodies to show their importance or to see them into the next life, and other objects were buried as a part of rituals or religious ceremonies.

What a load of rubbish

Then there was the biggest reason for burial: getting rid of domestic waste; all the rubbish people didn't want lying around, smelling the place out. Today, you put it in a bin-liner out for the dustmen. In pre-dustbin days, people dug a hole and, when it was full, filled it in. (A lot of our rubbish still ends up in landfill sites today, remember.) Domestic waste can tell the trained eye a great deal about a society. All of these things are examples of stuff that was supposed to be in the ground in the first place. It was even under soil way back when.

Cities under soil

Okay, so that may account for some of the smaller finds – coins, jewellery, gold and silver, weapons, rubbish and the suchlike – but that doesn't explain why whole cities have to be dug up. How did they get to be way below the surface?

The force of nature

One answer is a natural disaster. One of the most famous archaeological sites in the world is Herculaneum – a Roman port frozen in time or, to be more accurate, covered by volcanic lava in AD 79 (that's near enough two thousand years ago). It was once at ground level, and then the volcano created a new ground level on top of it!

It took early archaeologists and plenty of dynamite to first uncover it. (You can read more about the dastardly doings of early, treasure-seeking archaeologists at Herculaneum and Pompeii in the *Five famous finds* section, starting on page 78.)

Other natural disasters which covered human dwellings include: earthquakes, sandstorms, landslides and changes in water and sea levels. A river can become so silted up that it begins to silt the surrounding land and it's tough luck if you live there. Time to move!

Moving on

It's also worth remembering that, in the past, there were far fewer people living on this planet than there are now. Today, there are about six billion people in the world. In 1850 there were only 1.2 billion. Back in the days of William the Conqueror, there were just over 265 *million* – not billion – people and, if you go back as far as 10000 BC (which is around 12,000 years ago) there were probably only 4 million inhabitants. This means that hundreds of thousands of years ago, if your house fell into disrepair or you wanted to move, you could just leave it, build a new one and let nature take its course, unless you had a jolly good reason for staying.

Left to decay

The old dwelling would become victim to wind, rain, insects, fungus... and, eventually collapse. Plants grow between bricks and stones. Roof slates fall off. Timbers rot. Amazingly, in the right (or wrong, depending upon how you look at it) climate, a masonry – stone – building can disappear beneath the ground in under thirty years. As individual stones fall, the remaining roofless structure collects leaves and other debris creating ideal growing conditions for plants and trees, until much of the old building material helps to form the new soil itself.

Bigger and better

Yet another reason why many building remains are underground (and often *under* more modern buildings) is that human beings have always been striving to make things bigger and better. Most ancient towns and cities are built in particular areas for particular reasons; on top of hills for defence, by the mouths of rivers for trade, on the flatlands for farming, to give just three examples. These reasons for staying put remained good ones so, over the centuries, if people wanted new houses, they'd knock down the old ones, level them and build on top... often leaving the foundations and remains of the old ones beneath. Over time, the average ground level of a town or city became higher and higher and higher.

Up and up

At the site believed to have been the famous city of Troy – where, according to legend, the Greeks tricked its citizens into accepting the 'gift' of the wooden horse – there is evidence of at least eight different levels of occupation – in other words there are seven 'different' cities, from different, earlier periods under the top one!

In the Near East there are mounds named 'tells' by the experts. These tells were created by the rebuilding of houses, made by mud bricks, one on top of the other. Originally made from earth, these houses soon went back to being earth when replaced. In the city of Jericho, the tell is over 15 metres (60 feet) high! The word 'tell' actually comes from the Arabic for 'tall'. No wonder archaeologists have to dig so deep to study the past!

Follow the clues
WHERE TO START DIGGING

There are a number of obvious reasons why archaeologists might start digging in a particular place. These include the fact that:

1 artefacts have been discovered there – they've been ploughed up in a field, come across by someone taking their dog for a walk, or dug up by someone out with a metal detector, for example.

2 there are historical documents to suggest that there's something there – these could be anything from local deeds belonging to long-gone properties to detailed accounts of a building or battlefield (including pictures or plans).

3 there are physical remains of buildings above ground – one end of a ruined chapel, for example, might suggest that more of the chapel remains below the surface. What is now a barn may, on closer inspection, prove to have been an ancient dwelling at one time, and so on.

4 there are features in the landscape to suggest early human occupation – an archaeological surveyor will detect lumps and bumps which suggest early earthworks (human-made defensive ditches and mounds, burial barrows, etc.).

5 outlines are revealed by aerial photography. From the air, much of what is difficult to detect from the ground can be seen very clearly. In fields, for example, the walls of buildings beneath the soil often show up as a different colour to the surrounding soil, giving a really clear picture of the outlines of

Roman villas, old castles, manor houses, and so on. There can be a number of reasons for this:

- shadows show up more clearly from the air, exaggerating the lumps, bumps and outlines

- crops or soil surrounding buried walls sink lower than crops or soil on top of them

- crops or soil in old ditches, etc., sink lower than surrounding soil or crops

- what's beneath the soil affects the rate of growth of crops above – in other words, crops without old walls beneath them have better drainage and grow better

- areas with bad drainage (with stone work beneath) retain water more than surrounding soil and show up darker

6 construction workers – preparing the ground for a road, pipeline, sewer, house or office block, for example, dig a big hole in what turns out to be an archaeological site.

7 local place names and traditions hint at a specific past. For example, an area named 'Tylers Hill' for centuries may prove to be the site of a medieval tile factory!

This drawing (above), based on an aerial photo, clearly shows the outline of archaeological remains beneath the crops in the field. The cross section below shows how what's beneath the soil affects what's seen above

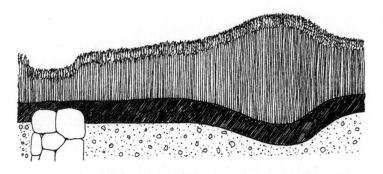

Getting down to business
EXPLORING THE SITE

Once a site has been located (whether deliberately or by accident), there's plenty of work that needs to be done before any digging takes place. Just because a site wasn't found as a result of historical research doesn't mean that no written records exist.

A historian is likely to be despatched to search local and national archives for information about the site. If it's a building, who built it? How much did it cost to build? Who lived there? When? Was it ever attacked? Was it ever visited by any famous people? (In Britain, many hotels and inns claim 'Queen Elizabeth I slept here', for example. (Well, she did get around quite a bit!) When was it destroyed? How? Why? These are all questions that can be answered in written documents though not, of course, in every instance. Sometimes only what's in the ground survives.

Useful written sources include:

old maps – showing before and after a property was built, thus helping to date it

records of birth, marriages and deaths – often naming the properties the people lived in

paintings and etchings – showing properties in various stages of their existence

court reports – mentioning disputes arising from the building of properties or the people living in them

list of building supplies – a wonderful source of information about a property now mainly gone

household accounts – giving an idea of the wealth of those who lived in the property, and their everyday needs and wants *histories of the area* – reporting events in and around the property, or those involving those who lived there

newspapers – a mine of information; and not just the reports and articles. Something as innocent as an early advertisement can reveal the location or the use of a property

tombstone and monument inscriptions – a really useful and accessible source of information about people and where they lived

To dig or not to dig?

That is the question. Just because the landscape has given away its secrets, some exciting artefacts have come to the surface, and written records have given a clue as to what might be down there, it doesn't automatically mean that the modern archaeologist will dig.

In the past, much 'archaeology' had as much to do with treasure-seeking and glory-seeking as trying to understand the past... if not more so. To know that there might be something exciting just waiting to be dug up meant dig,

dig, dig. Today, archaeologists weigh up the pros and cons very carefully indeed.

Sometimes decisions have even been made to leave things where they are until, hopefully, more advanced technology and techniques are invented to study them. Just because a site has been located doesn't instantly mean that someone needs to dig it up!

To answer a specific question

One reason for excavating – digging – at a particular site might be to answer a specific question, or questions, about the past. In other words, rather than digging away to simply see what's there, the whole way the dig is approached is to try to answer these questions. Some experts might decide, on this basis, that – if they think it unlikely they'll be able to find such answers at a particular site (which would benefit archaeologists everywhere and increase our understanding of days gone by) – the site should be recorded but left unexcavated.

Wait and see

Some other archaeologists have a totally different view. They believe that the beauty of excavations is that you never know, for sure, what you'll find. What starts as an excavation to uncover a Roman bath house could end up revealing an earlier Iron Age settlement underneath. Currently, the only sure-fire way of making these unexpected discoveries is by digging. They also argue that, in order to increase the skills of current archaeologists and train new ones, carefully planned digs are essential.

To the rescue!

With more and more house and road building throughout the world, as populations increase, one of the most common forms of excavations are 'rescue digs'. If building works are about to take place where an archaeological site has already been identified, archaeologists often find themselves digging and recording in a very limited time period – finding out as much about the site as possible – before the developers move in and the site is, possibly, lost for ever.

Salvage what you can!

If developers unexpectedly uncover ancient remains, and they're not deemed 'special' enough to prevent the site's destruction, a 'salvage excavation' has to be undertaken. Although archaeologists record as much information as they can, salvage digs really are a race against time and the highest of standards of a dig cannot always be met. It's a matter of saving what you can before the bulldozers come rolling back in.

Getting the go ahead

To be this near to digging, it's safe to assume that you've got your funding – excavating costs money – and you've got permission to dig. Funding usually comes from museums, universities, government, research trusts and even developers. Permission comes not only from the landowners and/or tenants but also local authorities and, in certain circumstances, central government. For example, in England, certain important sites are protected by English Heritage (once called the Department of Works). Even if they agree to let professional archaeologists investigate sites, they have the power to dictate where they can and cannot dig and even tell them how many trenches or how big an area can be excavated. An English Heritage official (usually an archaeologist) may also remain on site to observe.

Many archaeological sites are on farmland and everything has to be agreed from access to the site (which tracks the archaeologists can and can't use), to compensation for any loss of crops. No one said that arranging a dig had to be easy!

Choosing your team

Except in the rarest of rare situations, one thing you can be pretty sure of is that most archaeological digs include one big happy band of people: volunteers. Volunteers are the backbone of archaeological digs! A great deal of digging doesn't need specialists – though it needs specialist supervision – and volunteers are ideal for this. They work for the fun of it; in the more out-of-the-way sites it's often in return for food and accommodation (and for 'accommodation' read 'a place to pitch tent').

A volunteer can be anyone from an archaeology student to a keen amateur archaeologist to a sixth-former, with no archaeological experience, from school. Tasks will be assigned to them based on their abilities and experience and, in more straightforward excavations, they can make up the majority of the workforce.

Typical jobs for volunteers will include fieldwalking – walking across a field collecting fragments turned up by the plough over the years – along with straightforward digging and washing of finds.

Some very, very, very important digs, however, may include a whole raft of specialists from every field of archaeology: from experts on bones to experts on bugs; not to mention the whole 'back-up' team from security guards to cooks.

In some parts of the world, much of the 'donkey work' is done by cheap local labour – people who have other jobs but earn a bit of extra money working on sites. In places such as Egypt, with its extraordinarily rich archaeological history, many local people have built up and passed on vital skills of excavation and are of invaluable help to the professional archaeologist.

Different roles

Different archaeologists specialise in different periods of history or prehistory (the time before writing). For example, some archaeologists may be experts on the Bronze Age, others on the Middle Ages. Some may be able to identify a piece of pottery from the tiniest fragment, whilst another archaeologist may specialise in coins or burial mounds. The director of the dig

– the most senior archaeologist on site – may be in overall charge, but can't be an expert in everything so will be reliant on all of his or her team members for their skills.

Who's who?

Then there are the really specialised members of the team, with very specific scientific knowledge or skills. Here are just a handful of the specialists you might find on a dig – some working full-time, others simply called in when their area of expertise is needed – to give you an idea of just how diverse people's skills are, and how they combine to give the archaeologist as full a picture as possible of what went on and when.

dendrochronologist:
>an expert in dendrochronology, the dating of timber by taking core samples and comparing with existing samples of known ages (matching the ring patterns of the wood). *See pages 74–75.*

geophysicist:

an expert at using and interpreting data from resistivity meters and magnetometers; instruments used to survey archaeological sites by detecting what's below the surface. *See pages 32–37.*

forensic archaeologist:

one of a number of names for an expert in human remains; bone specialist, who can – in the right circumstances – identify a person's gender, diet, approximate age and cause of death from limited human remains.

environmental archaeologist:

an expert who can identify what the local environment must have been like from the insect and plant remains found on site. Even remains of food in a mummified stomach can sometimes be used to identify a region visited by the dead person.

archaeological surveyor:

a surveyor who specialises in interpreting

the landscape, identifying human-made features and changes in landscape over time.

Hidden depths

Sometimes, different kinds of specialist are needed. In the case of underwater archaeology, for example, this would include divers, submarine pilots and those able to pinpoint areas on seacharts rather than landmaps.

In theory, the approach to underwater archaeology – often called 'marine archaeology' if it takes place out at sea – is the same as the approach to archaeology on dry land... but with the obvious drawbacks of working underwater. For starters, divers can only stay beneath the surface for set amounts of time. Then there's the matter of equipment.

The satellite revolution

Once an excavation on dry land is underway, measurements can be made using a theodolite; a kind of small telescope, mounted on a tripod (three-legged stand), which is free to move both horiziontally and vertically. Underwater, however, archaeologists had to mainly rely on tape measures! Fortunately, this changed with the arrival of Global Positioning Systems, a method using a series of satellites orbiting the Earth which can work out the exact latitude, longitude and elevation (height) of any object, underwater or otherwise. Good news though that is, for the rest of the book, we'll be keeping our feet firmly on the ground, however muddy that may be!

The lie of the land

Before any earth is actually dug, it's important to have a contour survey drawn up. This will show the topography of the site. In other words, where every little lump or bump is on the surface. These are sometimes called 'earthwork plans'. To an archaeological surveyor, what shows up in a contour survey could hold important clues as to what might lie underneath and where best to dig test trenches.

Resistance is futile!

Another great help in getting an idea of what's under the ground, *before* a single spade-hole has been dug, is the work of the archaeological geophysicists. Geophysicists use two main types of equipment, both surveying instruments. These are the resistivity meter and the magnetometer.

The resistivity meter passes an electric current through the soil. The damper the soil, the easier the electricity flows through. (In other words, there is less resistance to the electricity or less electrical resistance.) The amount of electrical resistance is recorded. Filled-in pits have damper soil – and therefore less electrical resistance – than the undisturbed soil around them and soil above buried walls have the least dampness so show the most resistance.

The geophysicist walks back and forth, in a straight line, passing the resistivity meter over the entire site. The information recorded by the meter is then either plotted onto a map of the site by hand or fed into a computer and printed out on a scaled down version of the site, showing the driest areas darkest and the dampest areas lightest.

This printout of the geophysicist's findings using a resistivity meter clearly shows the dark outlines of what might be the outer walls of a building. The shape suggests a medieval church. The lighter readings (where the electrical resistance was least, so the soil dampest) could be graves

Magnetometer magic!

There are certain features which the magnetometer can pick up which the resistivity meter cannot. The only problem is that the magnetometer is more likely to be confused by surrounding items. For example, it's no good using a magnetometer in a heavily built-up area. If you use it near iron fences, electric trains, overhead power cables or even over igneous rock the results are interfered with and, therefore, useless. In those instances, a resistivity meter would have to be used.

A magnetometer works on the principle that buried objects – walls, iron objects, kilns, fire hearths – produce small variations (blips, if you like) in the Earth's magnetic field. For example, a grave containing a skeleton has greater magnetic susceptibility than the untouched soil around it, whereas a wall will have less magnetic susceptibility.

It doesn't matter if you're not 100% clear how it works, so long as you realise that these greater, lesser and normal magnetic readings can be recorded in different shades, so can help to build up a picture of the site.

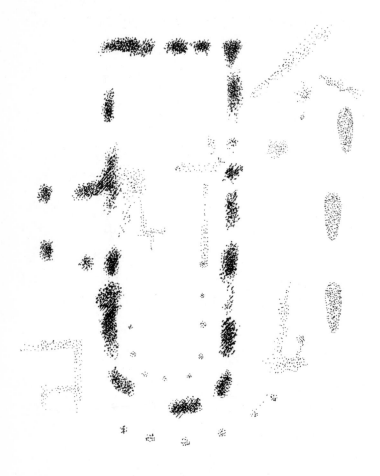

This printout is of the same site as on page 34, this time using the findings from a magnetometer. As with the resistivity meter, it shows the outline of the church and the graves. It also shows some other features not picked up by the resistivity meter

So which machine is better? Well, when it comes to trying to detect walls, roads and ditches, the resistivity meter comes first. But when it comes to pits and small iron artefacts – more isolated objects – the magnetometer wins. Where the resistivity meter comes out ahead, though, is that it's less bothered by interference, and thick vegetation. A site surveyed by a combination of both techniques would be a very well surveyed site indeed.

Metal detectors

I imagine that, round about now, some of you are asking 'what about metal detectors?'. Well, they can, indeed, give quick results as to where it might be worth digging for metal (though they can't 'read' as far below the soil as a magnetometer)... but most archaeologists are interested in excavating whole areas rather than where specific goodies might be found.

In fact, in the wrong hands, metal detectors can do a great deal of harm. Important archaeological information might be destroyed by someone with a metal detector digging up a metal find. Though the find in itself might not be important, the area around it might be, and ends up damaged by the digging.

Sometimes the find may be genuine 'treasure' and it is a great loss to the archaeological community that it has, in effect, been stolen. In many countries, most items found by unauthorised use of metal detectors don't belong to the 'finder', anyway, but to the landowner or the country, so keeping them is theft. To use a metal detector on a protected archaeological site without permission is, more often than not, against the law. Digging for treasure when a metal detector bleeps is not true archaeology but can be of assistance to the archaeologist when, say, sifting excavated soil for any finds which may have been overlooked.

The heart of archaeology
EXCAVATION

In my introduction, I referred to archaeologists as being detectives, using the clues they find to build up a picture of what happened in the past. The excavation site could, therefore, be thought of as the crime scene where everything must be studied very carefully because the most unassuming, 'unimportant' artefact might turn out to give a vital new clue as to how we used to live.

Some archaeologists, however, have described archaeological digs as being more like post-mortems. Instead of cutting up a corpse to find out as much as possible about the once living person, the archaeologist is dissecting the site to learn about what has gone on before. Either way, 'great care' is the key and the preparation and planning discussed in the previous chapter is vital.

Clearing the way

As we've seen, a proper dig takes time to prepare but, eventually, the planning is over, the site has been surveyed and the team is in place. Let the excavation begin! What happens first? Usually, this is removal of the modern layer covering the archaeology beneath it. In a field, this may just mean the thinnest of thin top soil – and even a small mechanical digger might do more harm than good. On an urban site, though, this could mean pulling down a whole modern building and shifting all the rubble... and a ball and chain, mechanical diggers and a fleet of dump trucks are needed! There's no such thing as a 'typical' archaeological site.

Putting the survey to the test

Sometimes an archaeological team may not have the time or the funds to excavate a whole site, so will put in a number of test trenches in places where they hope they'll be best suited to give them the information they're after, based on the contour survey. These trenches might be dug to try to answer anything from 'was there really a medieval church there?' to 'is this an ancient barrow – burial mound – or simply a natural feature?' to 'where was the boundary wall of the settlement?'

If a test trench reveals important information, it can be extended, or new ones opened up near it. If it comes up empty, it can be closed down... in other word, filled back in!

Tackling the site

The important question is what kind of an excavation have you planned for? What are you trying to achieve? If you're interested in a particular period or building – say a medieval monastery – and you want to find out as much about it as possible, you'd want to uncover the remains of all the buildings to get a clear idea of their layout: an overall plan of the monastery. These are called 'open excavations', because you'd be opening up the whole site.

If, however, you were on the same site, but were interested to find out whether the monastery was built on an earlier, pagan (pre-Christian) settlement, uncovering the whole plan wouldn't prove or disprove this. In this second example, it'd be more important to cut through the layers of soil (the deeper you go the further you go back in time) until you reach the section which contains the monastery and the sections beneath it, hopefully revealing the pagan settlement you believe to be there.

Two things at once

In an ideal world, every archaeological dig would reveal as much as one could possibly learn from a site. In the real world, the two approaches I've just described don't necessarily work too well together. Say, for example, you're not only interested in the possibility of the pagan settlement built before the monastery, but also anything built after the monastery (in other words, in the layers – the sections – above it)? You wouldn't want to clear away the soil above the monastic remains either... so how could another archaeologist get to see the whole layout?!

There are ways around this, of course, but it does help to demonstrate that a great deal of planning has to go into a dig before a single spade of earth is dug. The aims and objectives of the excavation and the methods to be used as a result have to be decided very carefully indeed.

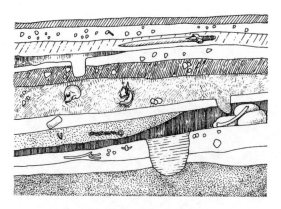

*A trench showing strata (layers of soil and their contents)
from various different periods*

Starting grid

One way to get around the strata versus open excavation problem was, to a certain extent, solved by Sir Mortimer Wheeler's grid system. The site was divided up into a grid of equal squares, and each square excavated leaving narrow unexcavated strips (called baulks) between them. This way, the archaeologists could get an overall view of what they were unearthing from the excavated squares, and study the chronological layers of remaining soil in the baulks.

Stage One of a grid excavation

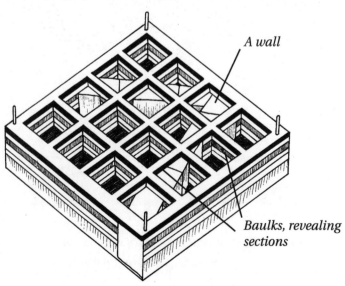

A wall

Baulks, revealing sections

Once all the information had been carefully recorded from these remaining strips of soil, these could then be removed to expose the whole site.

Stage Two of a grid excavation

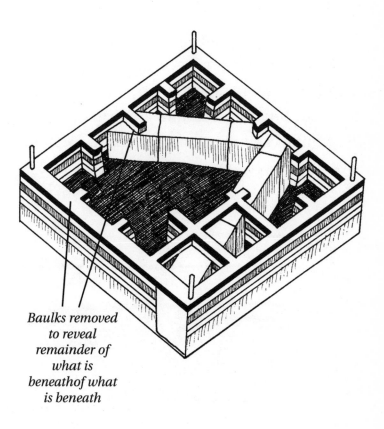

Baulks removed
to reveal
remainder of
what is
beneathof what
is beneath

The problem with this approach was that it was painstakingly slow and many of the baulks would be showing very similar information about the stratigraphy (layers of soil) anyway.

The more common approach

Today, more often than not, there's a compromise. Some deep and carefully positioned trenches may be dug and preserved so that the stratigraphy can be studied, whilst the rest of the site becomes an open one (with everything carefully cleared back and recorded, layer by layer, until the main structure is revealed).

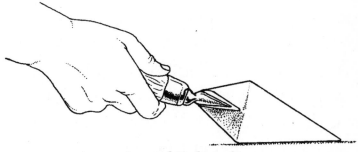

trowel in hand

All hands to the soil!

Whatever the approach decided on, the exciting moment in an archaeological excavation finally comes when the very top of the archaeological level has been reached. The dig really is under way. This is no place for diggers of the mechanical kind, it's a hands-on experience from here on in. Now the area must be scraped clear using hand tools; more often than not, the trusty hand trowel held at a slight angle.

Opposite page: an open site, uncovered section by section (layer by layer) to reveal 'the whole picture'. Although the vertical picture of layers is physically lost as digging goes on, it can be recorded and re-created in diagrams and in computer models

A tool for the job

At various stages, though, an archaeological dig can employ a whole raft of tools from huge earthmovers to the smallest of brushes used to clear away the tiniest amounts of soil before lifting an artefact from the ground. Even vacuum cleaners can come in handy when it comes to clearing small amounts of soil! And what happens to the great mounds of earth that are dug at the bigger excavations? In some instances, every single tonne of it is sieved to look for archaeological and environmental evidence. (Seeds, bugs, etc. can give clues as to the climate and vegetation of a site in the past.)

A colourful past

As the archaeologist scrapes away, s/he is very careful to note the different colours in the soil. These can help to tell a very important story, particularly about areas of the site that once contained wooden structures, which have long since rotted away to nothing. For example, a circle of darker soil could indicate the position of an old post hole. Uncover enough of them, and the archaeologist can begin to build up a picture of the structure that once stood there, supported by these posts. Dark patches might also reveal evidence of burning, requiring further investigation to determine whether the fire had been a hearth (for heating and cooking in the home) or a kiln (for 'firing' pots), for instance.

Being able to 'read' the soil in this way takes real training, skill and experience and shows why infinite care needs to be taken at this stage of the dig. Colour differences in soil can, to the trained eye, reveal everything from the smallest hole to great big defensive ditches.

Three archaeological features are revealed as three darker patches in the soil

Once excavated, they're shown to be three medieval graves, complete with skeletons

In black and white

Like everything else on the dig, these patches of colour will not only be recorded in colour photos, scale drawings and diagrams and in written notes, but in black and white photographs too. Why? Because black and white photographs can sometimes show up such differences more clearly and vice versa. Video photography is useful for recording the archaeologists at work – the methods they employ – as well as the discoveries they make. Photographic plans of the overall site (taken from above) are sometimes used instead of hand-drawn ones. This technique is called photogrammetry. Results can now be fed into computers, along with the contour survey, to create a three dimensional model of the site, which can be looked at from many angles.

Thinking of others

Whatever the method of excavation used and whatever artefacts are removed or left behind, archaeologists have a clear responsibility for other archaeologists and future generations to record as much information about their dig as possible. Sometimes, sites are returned to years later and trenches put in on the basis of information supplied by earlier archaeologists... If the record keeping is poor, this can lead to complications and frustration. (Amateur Victorian archaeologists were notoriously bad at specifics, so locating exactly where a sword was found or a wall unearthed can prove a nightmare for modern professionals!)

For the record

Recording what is unearthed, from the position of a wall to the exact location of where a brooch or human remains were found, is a vital part of any professional excavation. Once a dig is over, the site is usually covered with earth once more (for its own protection), but artefacts have been removed and strata destroyed. It'll never be as it was when it was originally discovered, so drawings, diagrams, photographs – both still and video – and written records of what were found are vitally important, because no two sites, even of similar structures, are ever the same.

True to form

Written records are useful because if there's a standard form-filling procedure used by most professionals everywhere, then it's easy for one expert to analyse another's reported findings. You simply fill in the form on site (either on paper or on a laptop computer). This information can then be available to other archaeologists, listing everything including the location of all findspots (which are – you guessed it – the exact spots where all artefacts were found).

SITE	CONTEXT RECORD	Context No	125
	Additional Sheets	Type	

Stratigraphic Matrix

Trench/Site sub-division	Overlies	Checklists (for Description):
	Butts	**DEPOSIT:**
	Cuts	1. compaction 2. colour
Group No	Fills	3. composition (over 10%) 4. inclusions
	Overlain by	5. tickness 6. extent 7. methods
Plan Nos	Abutted by	8. condition
	Cut by	**CUT:**
Section Nos	Filled by	1. shape in plan
	Same as	2. description of profile
	Part of	(shape of base and sides; break of slope at top/base)
Photographic	Consists of	3. dimensions 4. truncation
	Relationship uncertail	5. other comments
		MASONRY
		1. material 2. size of material
		3. finish 4. coursing and bonding
		5. form and faces

Description (see checklists)	Interpretation/Discussion

Finds none ☐ ceramic ☐ bone ☐ glass ☐ stone ☐ other ☐ please specify:

Finds Refs	Soil Samples	Recorder
		Date
Comments on finds		Checked

This example of a recording sheet is reproduced with kind permission of the Department of Archaeology, University College London

In the frame

When it comes to illustrated records, out comes the drawing frame. This is a wooden frame which measures a metre square from the inside edges (about 3 feet x 3 feet). It is strung with nylon string, top to bottom and side to side, to create 100 ten-centimetre squares.

The record keeper has a piece of paper with a similar grid drawn on it only, say, ten times smaller. In other words, each ten centimetre grid on the drawing frame is represented by a one centimetre grid on the paper. Now all s/he has to do is to place the grid on the area to be recorded and copy exactly what is positioned where.

This fairly straightforward process results in an accurate plan to a scale of 1:10 (i.e. one centimetre on the page represents ten centimetres in real life).

A drawing frame has been placed over an area covered with broken pottery. The location of each piece is being recorded onto the grid plan

Going potty

It obviously depends what kind of site you're digging as to what the most common artefacts are you'll find. If you're excavating a medieval tile factory, you might expect to find plenty of pieces of medieval tile, for example! There are, however, two types of artefact which regularly turn up in sites from different periods, built for different uses, and these are pieces of pottery and coins. Why? Because people have needed pottery vessels to keep things in ever since pottery was invented, and coins have been around for a long, long time too. In the UK, coins date back to Roman times.

Make a date

Fortunately for the archaeologist, both coins and sherds (broken bits of pottery) have something in common. They're relatively easy to date.

More modern coins actually have dates on them. Earlier ones might include an emperor or monarch's head on one side, and the dates of their rule in a particular region is known. Today, databases exist of thousands of coins and their dates against which a coin found at an archaeological site can be compared.

Pottery is so useful because people from different periods and different parts of the world made pottery in their own distinctive styles using the clay available to them. The shape of a lip of a pot – possibly determined from just a few sherds – will enable an expert to give a rough date as to when, and even where, the pot was originally made. Testing the contents of the clay might narrow the field down even further. Decoration on a sherd can also be an important clue.

Remember, even thousands of years ago, people were trading with each other. A pot found on an archaeological site was not necessarily made on site. It could have come from thousands of miles away and reveal important new information about trade and travel at the time.

Finds tray

Any volunteer who's worked on a dig is probably familiar with the phrase 'put it in the finds tray'. At first, you believe that every single piece of pottery or bone is probably of earth-shattering importance, so you keep calling over one of the archaeologists every time you find something that isn't just soil or an earthworm. Although these fragments will help to build an overall picture of the site, they can be safely placed in finds trays (which look suspiciously like flat plastic seed trays you see in garden centres), to be taken away, cleaned, identified and – where necessary – conserved later.

If a volunteer starts to uncover the hilt of a sword, part of a skeleton or a mosaic floor, however, all thoughts of the finds tray are forgotten and the true archaeologists take over the trench.

In the next chapter, we'll take a look at what happens to all sorts of finds.

A cloud on the horizon

I can't finish a chapter on excavation, however, without mentioning the one thing which affects an archaeological dig more than just about anything else. You guessed it – the weather. Whatever the time of year in the UK, for example, you never know if a sudden burst of rain will flood that lovely grave you've just unearthed... or soak that recently exposed soil, making it impossible to tell your post hole from a puddle! Grey, gloomy days don't offer the best conditions to identify and record the soil sections, either. But neither do dazzlingly bright ones, where the heat is drying out the soil too!

The obvious solution is to have portable shelter on standby in countries with such unpredictable climates. These can range from huge marquees, fixed in place, to tarpaulins pulled over smaller holes if and when the rain starts. Specially designed lightweight awnings can be carried onto the site to protect specific areas of excavation if it starts raining... which is all well and good so long as you don't get high winds!

Some of the most important sites in these areas are given a more permanent covering so that work can continue all the year round, whatever the weather.

Too dry!

At the other end of the scale, there are some parts of the world where the site's *dryness* is its problem. A water supply is vital for everything from drinks for the archaeologists to cleaning finds. I've said it before and I'll say it again: no one said excavating had to be easy!

Dealing with artefacts
THEIR IDENTIFICATION, DATING, CONSERVATION AND PRESENTATION

Some of the more basic processes of archaeology are very basic indeed! If you need to clean thousands of pieces of pottery and tile, covered in clumps of earth, there's nothing more effective than a line of volunteers on site, each with a washing-up bowl of water and a toothbrush. Nothing very glamorous there! If, of course, the water washes away the earth to reveal something possibly more important or fragile, then the artefact might be considered for more careful cleaning. They're usually supervised by the finds assistant. S/he is also responsible for bagging and labelling the finds, prior to their being treated or analysed further if needs be.

Some artefacts can be instantly identified and/or roughly dated the minute they come out of the ground. Others need to be thoroughly cleaned.

Marking finds, labelling bags and entering this information onto sheets (see page 53) is a vital part of dealing with finds. With some excavations coming up with literally thousands of sherds (pieces of pottery), it's vital that they – and their originally location – be easily identified.

Not my type

Finds have to be classified in as detailed a way as possible. I discussed pots at the end of the previous chapter, and they're a good example here.

Let's say we've managed to put together a

near-complete pot from various sherds found on site and it needs classifying. But how do we classify it? Its main classification might be POTTERY. But what was it made out of – this is where you hear such references as 'earthenware' pots, for example. Is the result fine, medium or coarse? How was it made? With or without a potter's wheel? Was it glazed? Was it fired in a kiln? Is the result well-fired or poorly fired?

Then, of course, there's the matter of the size of the pot and what it appears to be for. Does it have a handle and/or a spout? Did it once have a stopper in it? Could it have been a vase, a jug, a storage jar, a dish, a cup, a bowl. Sometimes it's easier to dismiss what a piece of pottery wasn't used for than to say, for sure, what it was!

The shape of things to come

The shape of a bowl – the width of its lip or the curve of its edge – can help an expert identify its age and origin (based on discoveries made previously). Designs and styles varied from place to place and changed over time. Typology is the study of how the design of objects change over time. This way a sequence can be built up to help date other artefacts.

All four of these artefacts are oil lamps, used in the same region. Over the years, as with fashion today, their design has changed. Their look gives a clue as to when they were made and used, though there were some overlaps in time. This is their typology

Before AD 90

AD 40 – 100

AD 70 – 200

AD 150 – 400

Sometimes – and excitingly – an artefact may be discovered that isn't quite like anything else, so its shape doesn't give the archaeologist all the clues s/he needs. So how can this particular object be dated?

Stratigraphy

A process used to help dating is called stratigraphy. This is based on the idea that, the deeper you dig, the 'further back in time' you're uncovering. You have a cross section of layers from different periods of history/prehistory and occupation.

There are problems with this approach alone, however, and it works best in association with typology. In other words, if your never-seen-anything-like-it brooch is found in the same layer as a piece of pottery that can be dated from its typology, then that will give you an approximate date for that brooch. (It could have been made earlier, but not later if in an undisturbed section – layer – of soil.)

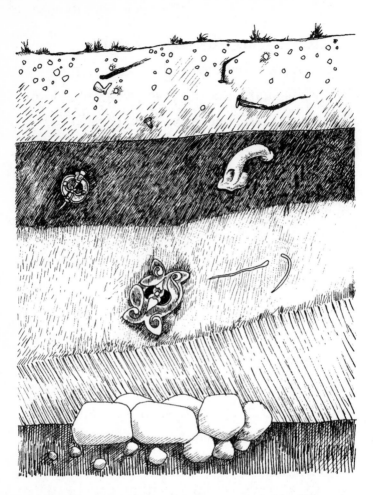

The archaeological site has been occupied by different people over different periods of history. It has different 'layers of occupancy', as this section shows. The unusual brooch, which typology alone could not date, was found in the same strata (layer) as a piece of pottery known, from typology, to be 12th century. By using stratigraphy and typology together, this suggests that the brooch is also 12th century

Making life difficult

If only life were that simple for archaeologists. What may, in one trench, appear to be an undisturbed layer of archaeology could have been interfered with by a growing tree root, a burrowing mole, rabbit, fox, ploughing or even someone laying a pipe, just metres away from where they've been digging. Stratigraphy is a useful tool in helping to date artefacts, but not an exact science.

A word to the wise

It's not just the shape of objects and the advance of technology that occurs over time but also language. Inscriptions carved or painted onto artefacts can be an invaluable help in attempting to date them. Quite apart from mentioning the reign of a particular monarch, they might also be written in a particular language. For example, think how different English today is compared to English of Shakespeare's day and, going back even further, to that of Chaucer. In other countries, written languages have changed altogether, giving additional clues to dating to the archaeologist. These kind of rough dating can be done on site. Other dating techniques often have to wait until artefacts are back in the laboratory, so we'll come to them later.

Conservation

It is usually once an excavation has been completed and the work of all those volunteers I referred to earlier is done, that archaeologists really begin to try to make complete sense of all that has been unearthed or removed.

This work generally falls into three categories. The first, and key, role is left to the conservators who, as their job title suggests, must do all they can to ensure that the artefacts are preserved in as good a condition as possible. They must also conserve them in a way that doesn't interfere with further scientific research (such as dating).

Artefacts such as bone, pottery, wood, stone, glass and leather can be washed in warm water.

Those such as metal, ivory, antler horn and unfired clay are best cleaned with sharp blades and equipment more familiarly used by dentists. Repeated washing of non-metals will usually remove harmful salts.

Even the method of drying cleaned objects is crucial. Most artefacts can simply be left to dry. Others, such as glass, need to be soaked in alcohol and ether before being dried, to avoid damage. Another approach is drying and consolidation; the removing of the water whilst, at the same time, replacing it with wax of 'PEG' (polyethylene glycol).

Metals are often x-rayed before cleaning to see whether corroded layers are hiding decoration. An x-ray can sometimes reveal that what appears to be a knobbly lump of corroded metal is hiding an exquisite artefact beneath!

Restoration

With conservation often comes restoration. In its simplest form, this is putting sherds back together to create as complete a pot as possible, or putting together bone fragments to re-create a skull. Whereas in the past gaps may have been filled with as closely matching material as possible – so that, at a glance – you couldn't tell old from new, it is more common practice today that gaps be filled with clearly different material. This way you're able to see what really is old, what was actually found.

Computer-generated images of an artefact in its complete, undamaged condition as fresh as the day it was first painted help to illustrate how an object once looked, as do modern-day replicas.

What have we here?

After conservation comes the job of getting as much information from the finds as possible. This covers everyone from plant specialists looking at the types of grain the people ate to environmentalists studying snails to determine climate and habitat. Objects are identified, dated and efforts are made to determine their origin. Was the pot made on site or brought by a trader from thousands of miles away? It is usually during this stage of the archaeological

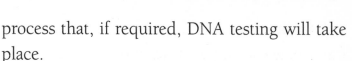

process that, if required, DNA testing will take place.

The building blocks of life

Every living cell contains a DNA molecule which contains the genetic instructions as to what that living thing is. In the case of a human being, it determines everything from colour of eyes to colour of skin and contains information about one's ancestors. By taking DNA samples from human remains, it is possible to determine a great deal about the person, when comparisons with existing DNA samples can be made – everything from relationships to other people, living or dead, and what part of the world they might have come from. This modern test has transformed the world of archaeology.

Radiocarbon dating

I expect those keen amateur archaeologists amongst you are asking yourselves 'when's he going to mention carbon dating?' And this is, indeed, another useful scientific tool, usually used once the dig is at an end. More properly called 'radiocarbon dating', here's how it works: all living things – people, plants, animals – absorb an invisible gas in the Earth's atmosphere called carbon dioxide, and retain (keeps) the element called carbon in them. There are three different types of carbon atom making three different varieties of carbon. These different varieties are called isotopes. The carbon isotope in carbon dioxide is called carbon-14. It's naturally radioactive, but the radioactivity is so weak that it doesn't harm anybody. The thing about radioactive material is that it decays over time at a set rate

In the late 1940s, an American called Willard F. Libby worked out that it takes 5,568 years for carbon-14 to decay to exactly half its original amount. (It later was revised to 5,730 years.) He also knew that when a person, animal or plant dies, it stops absorbing any more carbon dioxide and the carbon-14 it has already retained starts to decay. Because he had worked out the rate of decay, by measuring the amount

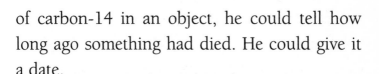

of carbon-14 in an object, he could tell how long ago something had died. He could give it a date.

Like any new test, there were teething troubles along the way and methods had to be improved. Also, he and his team needed large samples to come up with decent results. Today, experts can use as little as 5 milligrams. There are, however, still anomalies/glitches/errors with radiocarbon dating results and it shouldn't be assumed to be a 100% perfect dating method on its own.

Other dating techniques

Something called F-U-N dating can be useful. These are really three different dating techniques which, when combined, can give very accurate results. The 'F-U-N' comes from the three different techniques, one measuring levels of fluorine, another uranium and another nitrogen. Changes in the levels of these elements are affected by such things as temperature and moisture in the air. This means that they can be used to work out whether, for example, bones found together are contemporary with each other – from the same time – because the rate of changes of the F-U-N levels should be the same, if they've been through all the same local changes in climate.

Another technique is thermoluminescence dating. This is a brilliant aid to archaeologists because it can date pottery and – with sherds, sherds, sherds, everywhere – that's fantastic! It can date a pot made as long as 70,000 years ago... but it is of limited accuracy in some cases. Like all dating techniques, it's best to use it alongside other methods, to build up an overall picture of a date. It's based on the amount of light and energy released from a fired clay object when heated.

Then, as discussed elsewhere, timbers in a building can be dated using a process called dendrochronology. A sample, or 'plug', is taken and the growth rings are compared to a database of trees of known ages. When a match is found – rings from different years are of different widths, creating a kind of fingerprint - an age can be given. The danger here is that you're dating the original tree, not when the timber was used. For example, 500 year-old timbers could have been used to build a house ten years ago! Dendrochronology, however, is a particularly good way of determining if something *isn't* as old as it seems by proving the wood is from a tree of a later period than fits in with the supposed date of a building.

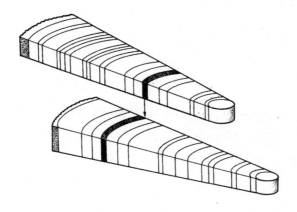

The variations in tree-ring widths in a given area (affected by the same harsh winters and hot summers) means that trees of different ages can be arranged in an overlapping sequence to build up a bigger picture of the ring patterns in an area, against which samples can be matched and dated. This is dendrochronology

And, finally?

The archaeological site has been discovered and surveyed. Background research has been carried out, approval has been given to dig, funds raised, a team assembled, an approach agreed upon and work has got underway. The excavation is now complete, the site covered, and artefacts and soil samples labelled, bagged and tagged. The finds have been preserved, cleaned, analysed and, in certain instances, restored. What now? Now the archaeological director and her/his team bring together all the different pieces of information they've gathered and write up a report placing the significance of their discoveries in the context of the period of history or prehistory into which it fits. They give everything a meaning. A sense of place. And the artefacts? Most are stored behind the scenes in universities, laboratories and museums throughout the world. Some of the finer or more unusual pieces are put on display.

Sharing knowledge and excitement

Some people greet the word 'museum' with a

groan of despair, even though museums have come a long way from being dimly lit rooms with nothing more than dusty glass case after glass case... but even those dusty glass cases held some amazing finds. A museum is an opportunity for us, the public, to see items dating back thousands of years, belonging to everyone from fabulously rich pharaohs to ordinary people, going about their lives since human beings first set foot on this earth. These, along with reconstructions of places and ways of life, are the legacy of the archaeologist; helping us have a better understanding of ourselves and how we used to live.

Five famous finds

FIVE GREAT ARCHAEOLOGICAL DISCOVERIES

1. POMPEII & HERCULANEUM

Vesuvius erupts!

On 24th August AD 79, the volcano Vesuvius erupted. The explosion not only sent thousands of tonnes of lava pouring on top of the Roman port of Herculaneum, but also covered the nearby town of Pompeii with seven metres of ash and stone. Two days later, the town was deserted. Those who could, fled. The two thousand or so who remained were killed. Over time, trees and vegetation grew over the ash-covered town. It became farmland and Pompeii's whereabouts was eventually forgotten.

So close

Pompeii came close to being discovered as far back as 1593 when the owner of a villa at Torre Annuziata wanted grand fountains. The fountains needed a water supply, so an underground tunnel needed to be dug. His workmen dug right down into Pompeii and discovered a few artefacts. But the villa owner wasn't interested. He thought they were simply remains from an old Roman villa – and there were plenty of them about – and his fountains were far more important!

Blasted treasure seekers

Despite being under 24 metres of lava which

hardened into solid rock, the port of Herculaneum was actually uncovered before Pompeii. In 1738, an engineer called Chevalier Alcubierre was put in charge of trying to excavate it. His main tools were pickaxes and gunpowder, digging tunnel after tunnel. (He was probably more interested in finding riches than preserving the past.)

Interest aroused

Now that Herculaneum had been discovered there was renewed interest in Vesuvius's eruption in AD 79, and the hunt was on to find the lost city of Pompeii. Alcubierre was put in charge of this 'dig' too and, in March 1748, some interesting finds were made. Pompeii had definitely been located. Unfortunately, Alcubierre caused a great deal of damage on this site too.

A series of advances

Later, a Swiss called Karl Weber took over. He was an architect rather than an engineer, and carried out very carefully planned excavations, limiting the damage as much as possible and keeping well-written records. His work was taken over by a Spaniard named Francesco La Vega. In 1860, Giuseppe Fiorelli became the man in charge, and it is to him that we owe the debt for preserving Pompeii. Though Fiorelli's good work has been carried on by others until this day, it was his methods that inspired and determined how this town under the ashes be preserved.

A street in Pompeii today, as it was almost 2,000 years ago before the disaster

A snapshot in time

Today, visiting Pompeii is like going back in time; but to a very specific time: the time that the burning ash and rocks came, killing many of its townspeople. Over the years, these people's bodies rotted away to nothing – we're talking about an event which happened almost 2,000 years ago, remember – leaving perfect people-shaped holes in the ashes where they'd once been. Firorelli had the inspired idea of pouring liquid plaster of Paris into the holes before clearing the ash. The plaster hardened and he now had 'statues' made from the moulds of once-living people.

Amazing details

The streets and houses of Pompeii and Herculaneum have given us many insights into life in Roman towns at the time. In Pompeii there's even a mosaic carrying the warning – in Latin – to 'Beware of the Dog'. You can see stepping stones across the road to avoid the mud and muck, wall paintings and the incredible plaster figures. They're not all of humans. One is of a dog, writhing in agony as the hot volcanic ash fell.

2. TUTANKHAMUN

A chance in a million

One of the most famous archaeological finds in the 20th century was the tomb of the Egyptian boy-king Tutankhamun, jam-packed with fabulous treasures. It was discovered in 1922, many years after it was assumed that there were no more riches to be discovered in Egypt's Valley of the Kings. The excavations began in 1912, led by the archaeologist Howard Carter. He was funded by George Herbert, better known as Lord Carnarvon.

A door!

After years of painstaking archaeology, local men working on the dig uncovered sixteen stone steps leading down to a sealed doorway. The date was 4th November 1922, and Howard Carter sent Lord Carnarvon a brief telegram, describing it as a 'wonderful discovery'. No efforts were made to enter the tomb until Carnarvon had arrived.

'Can you see anything?'

On his arrival, the first door was opened. They found a dark corridor filled with rubble which had to be cleared away before they could reach a second door. When this was finally reached, it was discovered to be sealed with Tutankhamun's name. On 26th November

1922, with Lord Canarvon right behind him, Howard Carter removed some stones from this doorway and looked into the tomb by the light of a single candle. 'Can you see anything?' asked Carnarvon. 'Yes, it is wonderful,' replied Carter.

It was some time before one could see, the hot air escaping caused the candle to flicker, but as soon as one's eyes became accustomed to the glimmer of the light the interior of the chamber gradually loomed before one, with its strange and wonderful medley of extraordinary and beautiful objects heaped upon one another.

Amazing artefacts

Tutankhamun's tomb was crammed with an extraordinary number and variety of artefacts, many of them fabulous riches and most of them designed to help the dead king be comfortable in the Kingdom of the West (the 'next life' for ancient Egyptians). There was everything from a throne and a bed to the small shabti figures who were supposed to come alive and do all his work for him. Perhaps the most impressive finds, though, were covering the actual body. Tutankhamun was wearing a solid gold mask and lying in a solid gold coffin!

The boy-king's golden death mask

Coincidence or curse?

Over the years, stories have built up that there was a curse written on one of the seals on the door of Tutankhamun's tomb, warning that entering would cause bad luck... I don't personally believe in curses, but here are just some of the strange things that are said to have happened to some of those involved in the dig:

 Howard Carter's pet bird was eaten by a cobra the very day the tomb was opened. There is a carving of a cobra on Tutankhamun's death mask.

 Lord Carnarvon died after a sudden illness, possibly caused by a mosquito bite on his cheek. X-rays of Tutankhamun's gold mask revealed a weakness in the metal in a similar place on its cheek.

An expert, on his way to x-ray the bones inside Tutankhamun's mummified body, died.

 When Carnarvon himself died, all the lights went out in the Egyptian city of Cairo and – at exactly the same time back in England – his dog gave a howl and died too.

 Of the 26 people at the grand opening of the tomb, six of them were dead within ten years.

I should point out, though, that some of those present weren't the youngest of people and, anyway, that means 20 out of 26 lived *beyond* the ten years, including Howard Carter himself! Curse or no curse, Tutankhamun, his tomb and the treasures within it is one of the most exciting archaeological finds of all time.

3. THE CITY OF TROY

The legend of Troy

Long ago, when the gods ruled from Olympus and walked the Earth, a soldier named Paris kidnapped Helen of Greece, the most beautiful woman in the world. He took her to the city of Troy where, due to the trickery of the gods, she fell in love with him and became Helen of Troy. Outraged, an army of Greek heroes surrounded the walled city and laid siege to it. But the people of Troy would not surrender. One morning they awoke to find the Greeks gone and a huge statue of a wooden horse outside the gates. Thinking it might be a peace offering, they opened the city gates and wheeled it inside. That night, a group of Greek soldiers, hidden inside the horse, crept out of it and opened the gates to let their comrades into the city. The Greek army burnt Troy to the ground.

The legend of Schliemann

A legend is a familiar story based on true events and involving real people from the past, which has been built upon and exaggerated over time. Although Heinrich Schliemann, a German archaeologist born in 1822, didn't necessarily believe the parts about the gods and heroes, he believed that Troy itself existed and had been destroyed. He'd first read the story when he was eight and swore that, one day, he'd find the city! When he grew up, most experts believed that Troy was sited in a place called Bunarbashi but, using information in the text of Homer's version of events, he decided it must be in Hisarlik. It was here he dug in the 1870s and here he found a city.

The city had been rebuilt many times, each

time on top of the previous occupation. He not only found evidence that the city had once been burnt to the ground but he also found fabulous treasure. He, and the world, was convinced he'd found Troy!

The truth is out there

The legend of Schliemann is as much a legend as the story of Troy and the wooden horse: it changed with the telling. This was Schliemann's own version of events, 'improved' over time. Schliemann was forever writing journals, keeping notes and sending people long letters, but he never recorded having read the legend of Troy as a child and swearing to find it. Funny that. He only wrote about Troy after he'd visited Hisarlik. Some of the land there, where Schliemann's excavations were later to take place, was owned by a man named Frank Calvert. Calvert was convinced that this was the location of the real Troy and told Schliemann so! More likely than not it was *he* who interested Schliemann in the history of Troy and convinced him that this was the right site. But Schliemann's 'bending of the truth' did not stop there.

Priam's Treasure

According to the Schliemann legend – in other words, his colourful version of events – he and his wife found a hoard of gold and silver on the site one day, which he named 'Priam's Treasure' after a king of Troy. Unfortunately for Schliemann, the records clearly show that his wife, Sophie, wasn't even on the site the day they supposedly 'found' the treasure together. There are now a number of theories as to where this 'treasure' actually came from; some more charitable than others:

- that the gold and silver was from the site, but collected together from unreported finds to make one, big exciting find (which would be much more attention-grabbing)

- that the site had been 'salted' with artefacts taken from Schliemann's other archaeological digs (because it would be much more sensational to find them in 'Troy')

- that the treasure was made up of forgeries: fakes.

Though the last may seem the most shocking, the others are equally appalling by modern archaeological standards. To fail to make accurate records as to where artefacts were genuinely found on site, just to make up a big hoard, destroyed valuable information to help with the understanding of the site.

To take the artefacts from another site not only gave Hisarlik a false history but also deprived the unidentified site from which they were taken of valuable information as well as the artefacts themselves.

Whatever Schliemann did, it's generally accepted, now, that he didn't tell the truth. At the time, however, his version of the discovery of Troy and its treasure was a worldwide sensation, and it helped to make the idea of archaeology even more popular than before.

Schliemann took photographs of his wife wearing some of Priam's Treasure. He published these, along with his version of events, in a book that was to sell worldwide

Remarkable twists and turns

Although you'll find a modern wooden horse at the archaeological site at Hisarlik today, there's still no absolute proof that this was Troy. Although one of the eight layers of occupation was burnt as both Homer's version and Schliemann claimed, it was from the wrong time period to have fitted with Homer's epic poem. Even more intriguing, though, is what happened to Priam's Treasure.

More stories and an amazing truth

When Heinrich Schliemann died in 1890, he left Priam's Treasure to a museum in Berlin. During the Second World War, the museum was bombed and a new legend was born: that of the melted treasure flowing down the steps of the museum in a waterfall of gold and silver. The truth be told, it – along with other national treasures – was being hidden somewhere far more weird and wonderful: in a building at Berlin Zoo! At the end of the war, Berlin surrendered to the Russian Army and Priam's Treasure ended up where it is today: in the Pushkin Museum in Moscow. The Germans want it back. So do the Turks. They claim that these artefacts – whatever their extraordinary history – should never have left Turkey in the first place.

4. THE ROSETTA STONE

A chance discovery

Not all important archaeological finds are made by archaeologists. This one was made by a soldier but, fortunately for us – and for Egyptologists in particular – this soldier realised that what he'd found might just be of some significance. How right he was! The soldier was a French one; a member of Napoleon's army in Egypt. The find was a large slab of stone, set in an old wall. It had writing all over it.

A place of safety

It was August 1799 and members of the French Engineers were building Fort Julien, near the town of Rashid. One of the officers overseeing the work was Pierre Bouchard. He later described how he saw a black stone, covered in inscriptions built into an old wall already on the site. Knowing Napoleon's fascination for all things ancient Egyptian, and seeing that there was more than one script (written language) on the stone – which made it unusual – he reported his finding to his superior officer, General Menou. The general agreed that the stone might be of interest, and ordered that it be removed to the French-held Egyptian city of Alexandria, for safekeeping.

A possible key?

The stone turned out to be part of a stela (an upright commemorative plaque, usually carved with writing), dating from 196 BC. There were three different forms of writing on it: Egyptian hieroglyphs at the top, a script that looked something like a form of Arabic in the middle and ancient Greek at the bottom. The French scholar had no problem translating the Greek and guessed that it was a translation of the other two languages. At that time, no one could understand the incredible ancient Egyptian hieroglyphs, carved into, or painted onto, every temple wall, obelisk, tomb, sarcophagus... just about everywhere throughout the country. Could this stone somehow be the key?

Jumping ship

Things weren't going too well for the French in Egypt, whose fleet had been defeated by English ships under the command of Nelson at the Battle of the Nile. When they finally surrendered, the French scholars made plans to sneak the stela – now called the Rosetta Stone after the old name for the town of Rashid, near which it was found – onto a French ship and home. But the English had realised the importance of the stone (rubbings of which had been sent out of Egypt for other scholars to see) and a General Tomkins Turner arrived with a military detachment to claim it... which is how the stone comes to be in the British Museum today.

French victory at last!

Despite the fact that the English physically owned the stone and an Englishman named Thomas Young made some important connections, it was a French scholar called Jean François Champollion who actually managed to decipher all the writing and, therefore, cracked the code to understanding ancient Egyptian hieroglyphs everywhere. He published his finding in 1824, having been the first human being to be able to read ancient Egyptian hieroglyphs in one-and-a-half-thousand years. (The Arabic-like script in the middle had turned out to be demotic, another – later – ancient Egyptian script.) The Rosetta Stone had been a passion to him, ever since he first saw the copies, taken by French scholars, when he was just eight years old.

Why such a great find?

Without the Rosetta Stone we may never have been able to understand the meaning of the hieroglyphs or, at least, it would have taken many more years to decipher them. It is the understanding of hieroglyphs that led to the creation of modern Egyptology and an understanding of the ancient Egyptians' gods and goddess, myths and legends, rituals and ceremonies. They were all written down there, in their beautiful script, for us to see but, before the stone was discovered and deciphered, they meant nothing to our modern eyes!

A final revelation

Cleaned in 1999, to commemorate the two hundredth anniversary of its discovery, the Rosetta Stone gave up another secret. It isn't naturally black at all (even though that's how it still appears on most T-shirts, mugs, mouse mats, jigsaws, scarves and ties, etc.). It is actually a beautiful veined pink stone, with a quartz-like sparkle in places.

5. THE CAVES AT LASCAUX

Four boys and a dog

Another French find, this time in France, was also made quite by chance and, again, not by archaeologists. In this instance, it was made by four teenage boys and a dog. It was 12th September 1940 – a year into the Second World War – and Marcel Ravidat, Jacques Marsal, George Agnel and Simon Coencas and his fox terrier were out walking in the woods on Lascaux hill near their village of Montignac. The thing about fox terriers is that, given the chance, they love dashing down fox holes or rabbit burrows. But, on this incredible day, he went down the biggest hole of his life!

To the rescue

A few years earlier, a large pine tree had fallen over making a hole in the ground near the heart of the wood. It was down this hole that Simon's dog now disappeared. The boys went to his rescue and found themselves in a narrow crevice with a large pile of rocks at the bottom. They were in a cave, with the rocks blocking what must once have been the original entrance.

World of wonder

They entered what is today known as the 'Great Hall of the Bulls' – and small wonder. The walls were covered in stunningly lifelike, bright prehistoric paintings of bulls, stags, horses and cows... some running, some swimming across a river, others chased by hunters with spears. But the caves didn't end there. Other walls revealed a series of pictures – thousands of years old, long before the days of writing – now called 'Scene of the Dead Man', including that of a man with a strange bird's head. The boys had discovered some of the most important prehistoric cave paintings ever found (with a little help from a dog).

What next?

They couldn't contain their excitement, of course, and the next day the local villagers came to take a look. Soon the rest of the world wanted a look-see! These included some of the top archaeologists of the day, one of the earliest and most famous being Abbot Henri Breuil. A number of caves inhabited by prehistoric people have been discovered in France, but those at Lascaux are some of the finest in the world. The war ended in 1945, and they became a tourist attraction.

Some of the magnificent cave paintings at Lascaux

Drastic action

With the rubble cleared and the entrance opened, the atmosphere in the caves was altered. Add to that the breath of the thousands of visitors, and the air became much damper than before. It caused the once vibrant colours of some of the prehistoric paintings to fade. Some even began to disappear. A decision had to be made based on archaeological importance rather than tourism. In 1963, the caves were closed to the public. Preserving this important archaeological find was rightly considered more important than people getting a chance to see it.

A FABULOUS FAKE!
THE PILTDOWN MAN

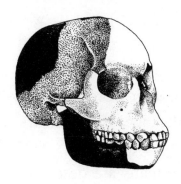

The missing link

What started out as being thought to be one of the greatest archaeological finds of all time turned out – many years later – to be nothing more than an ingenious hoax. The

Piltdown Man, a skull thought to be the missing link between human being's ape-like ancestors and modern-day humans, caused a sensation on its discovery in 1912. Today, the Piltdown Man is the name of a pub in Sussex, and an embarrassing footnote in archaeological and evolutionary history.

Darwin's evolution revolution

In 1859, Charles Darwin wrote a book called *On the Origin of the Species by Means of Natural Selection*. In it, he stated his belief that human beings and apes probably had an ancestor in common. (In other words, if you went back far enough in the ape and human's family tree, they'd share a relative.) That's NOT the same as saying that humans are descended from apes, by the way, which is a common error people make. Ever since most scientists came to agree with Darwin's theory, people were on the lookout for archaeological evidence to support it; they wanted to find this missing link between humans and apes.

An amazing package

In 1912, the British Museum in London received a package from a lawyer in Sussex who, by coincidence, had a very similar name to Darwin's. He was Mr Charles Dawson. The package contained part of a skull and jawbone which caused immediate excitement at the museum. The skull was human-like and the jawbone ape-like. A human skull with an ape-like jaw! Did this belong to that missing ancestor of both the ape and human? Was this the first real archaeological proof of the missing link?

A very British skull

Mr Dawson claimed to have found the skull, with its unique jaw, in a gravel pit in Piltdown, Sussex. That such a find should be found in England further delighted the British experts, who were probably rather jealous of the amazing prehistoric finds that had already been made in France! Over the next few years, Dawson worked alongside Sir Arthur Smith

Woodward from the British Museum and they uncovered more 'finds' from the pit.

The truth comes out

As time went on, discoveries of early humanoid remains in other places made the Piltdown Man seem strangely out of place, but it was science which finally exposed the 'find' for the fake that it was. It was discovered that both the skull and the jaw had been stained to look older, and that the teeth on the jawbone had been filed down to look more human-like. Eventually, the skull was identified as being 15th century (rather than over 100,000 years old) and the jaw as having come from an orang-utan. The hoaxer had put together an old human skull and a modern ape jaw, with filed down teeth, in an area salted with fossilised animal bones from the correct period of prehistory! It had taken until 1953 – over forty years since the Piltdown Man's discovery – to prove this missing link a fake.

A mystery to this day

What *hasn't* been established is who the hoaxer was. The most obvious suspect is, of course, Charles Dawson, the Sussex lawyer who claimed to have found the skull and sent it to the British Museum, but this is by no means certain. Sure, he might have been skilled enough to locate a skull and jawbone and to doctor them and 'age' them, but where would he have got all the other genuine fossils that were found in the pit to add credibility to his story... and why would he have done it?

There are some people who suggest that the hoaxer must have been a scientist, and a scientist with access to existing finds. The forgery – by 1912 standards – was a good one, and the fossils found with it were convincing corroborative evidence. But who? It seems unlikely that Sir Arthur Smith Woodward, himself, placed them there to be discovered and make his name.

A popular suggestion is that either Sir Grafton Elliot Smith or Professor William Sollas might have been behind the hoax. Both were rivals of Sir Arthur Smith Woodward and, it's suggested, would have been happy to discredit him and his work: exposing the hoax and ridiculing him for believing it...

The big problem with *this* theory, though, is that neither man did reveal the hoax or ridicule Smith Woodward, so the mystery as to whom the hoaxer really was remains just that: a mystery!

Secrets of the dead

THREE PRESERVED BODIES

1. KING RAMESSES

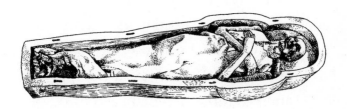

Magnificent in life

Think of a well-preserved dead body and you probably think of an ancient Egyptian mummy. After all, bodies were mummified for the very reason of preservation in the first place, weren't they? One of the most famous ancient Egyptian kings was Ramesses II. He ruled for 67 years, had over 200 children (outliving his twelve oldest sons) and is said to have died at the ripe old age of 90! His face was carved on numerous monuments across Egypt, including at the fabulous temple of Abu Simbel.

Fascinating in death

Today, Ramesses II's body lies in the Cairo Museum. The bandages have been removed from his body and you can gaze at the face of a man who lived over 3,000 years ago. This is partly thanks to the skill of the original ancient Egyptian embalmers and partly thanks to the skill of French scientists in the 1970s. A fungus was found to be eating away at the body and it was French experts who managed to put a stop to it.

2. TOLLUND MAN

Nature's pickling jar

It's not just humans who preserve things by pickling them. Nature can be a great pickler too! Peat bogs can act like giant pickling jars. If there's a human body in such a bog, the spongy top layer of peat can stop the air getting at it. It's the micro-organisms in the air that cause bodies to decay. No air means no micro-organisms which, in turn, means no decay. The body in the peat bog does not rot away. Over time, the bog stains the body brown and the skin becomes leathery but, apart from these minor changes, a thousand-year-old body discovered in a peat bog tomorrow could look much like the person the day s/he died, down to the hairs on their legs!

A nasty end

One of the most famous bodies found in a bog is Tollund Man. He was unearthed in the Tollund area of Denmark by two peat cutters – hence his name. Like many bodies discovered in bogs, Tollund Man's features have been squashed by the weight of the bog over the years. Noses don't contain bone, just cartilage which becomes soft and squidgy, but his features look stunningly peaceful. In fact, he had been garrotted – strangled.

Questions! Questions!

The question remains whether he was a murder victim, some kind of sacrifice or on the receiving end of some official Iron Age justice? He was buried with nothing except a leather cap and animal-hide belt. Using the tiniest amount of his hair, the latest carbon dating tests have suggested that Tollund Man lived in the very early Iron Age – about 400 BC – making him almost 2,500 years old! His remarkably preserved body can be seen at the Silkeborg Museum, just a few miles from where he was found.

3. OTZI, THE ICEMAN

One of the best preserved natural mummies is the Iceman found in a glacier near the Austrian-Italian border in 1991 by two German climbers. He was so well preserved that he looked like he could have been trapped in the ice just days before... if it wasn't for his grass cape and bow and arrows. Unlike those of Egyptian mummies and peat bog people, even his eyeballs were preserved. His body was tattooed.

A gathering of scientists

Dr Konrad Spindler of Innsbruck University headed a group of over one-hundred-and-fifty scientists from all over the world, who studied the body, clothes and equipment of the Iceman. It was discovered that he was over 5,000 years-old. With both the Austrian and Italian governments wanting to lay claim to this truly remarkable archaeological find, it was also established that the Iceman had fallen from what is now the Italian side of the mountain, in what was probably a hunting accident but which could have been murder.

Through the ages

DIFFERENT AGES IN ARCHAEOLOGY

Human prehistory – the time before writing – was originally divided into three periods (the Stone Age followed by the Bronze Age and then the Iron Age) by Christian Thomsen, first curator of the National Museum of Denmark.

The Stone Age was the period when people used stone (flint) tools. The Bronze Age was when they first used metals (bronze) and the Iron Age was when they'd discovered how to make iron; a much stronger and more useful material.

Prehistoric peoples could now be categorised

by the weapons and tools they used, rather than being lumped together as simply 'prehistoric'.

Ages and ages

When using archaeological terms such as 'Stone Age' and 'Iron Age' it is impossible to give them hard-and-fast dates, as though they were set periods in time, like 'Tudor England' or 'the Crusades'. They simply refer to times when people were using different types of tools made from different kinds of material: stone, bronze and iron. They represent periods of *development*; of moving from one technology to another. And different people in different parts of the world developed – went from one 'age' to another – at different times. It's only logical that people in a place where raw materials, such as iron ore, was in plentiful supply were more likely to start making tools from iron (and entering *their* Iron Age) long before people where iron was scarce and had to be traded. What is consistent, however, is the order in which development took place: stone, bronze and then iron. Here then are the key ages, and some of their dates:

STONE AGE:

Old Stone Age: Palaeolithic

- **AFRICA:**

  the Stone Age could have begun as far back as 2.5 million years ago

- **ASIA:**

  it probably began about 1.8 million years ago

- **EUROPE:**

  as recently as 1 million years ago. Ended round about 13,000 BC (15,000 years ago)

Middle Stone Age: Mesolithic

Around 13,000 BC the Earth's weather changed, food became more plentiful and a wider variety of tools were developed.

New Stone Age: Neolithic

About 8,000 BC farming began to take off, requiring new tools (not just those used for hunting and protection). People were settling down to live and farm in one place, rather than keeping on the move, hunting and gathering their food.

BRONZE AGE:

- **THAILAND:**
  began around 4,500 BC

- **GREECE:**
  about 3,000 BC

- **CHINA:**
  about 1,800 BC
  Ended around 1,200 BC (3,200 years ago)

IRON AGE:

The hardest to pin down of all the 'ages'. Though it started in some places round about 1,200 BC, the use of iron developed at wildly different times in parts of the world, amongst different cultures.

Archaeological terms

A GLOSSARY

barrow ancient burial mound

conservation methods of conserving archaeological remains (from human to building materials) so that they stay in a good stable condition

crop marks differences in crop growth, colour and height to suggest archaeological remains beneath the soil

dendrochronology the dating of wood from tree ring samples, compared to a database of trees of known ages

DNA deoxyribonucleic acid. Every living – or once living – cell contains a DNA molecule. This molecule, in turn, contains all the 'instructions' as to the characteristics of the living things. DNA tests on human remains can, for example, reveal the deceased's relationship to other remains found nearby

Egyptologist an archaeologist specialising in the study of ancient Egypt, including its language

fieldwork all outdoor archaeology, including the search for sites

findspots spots where artefacts were found

flotation method of separating pollen and seeds (wanted for analysis) from soil by mixing in water

F-U-N dating three dating techniques, measuring levels of fluorine, uranium and nitrogen, often used together

geophysics the study of physical properties of the Earth which archaeological geophysicists use to locate and plot buildings and objects beneath the soil, and to apply dating methods

grid excavations devised by Sir Mortimer Wheeler, where the site is initially excavated in equal squares, leaving narrow unexcavated strips for the *stratigraphy* to be studied

high status important buildings or objects, rather than those used for everyday purposes by 'ordinary' people

industrial archaeology the study of more recent industrialised sites (mills, mines, canals, railways, etc.) and the changes they brought to how we lived

living museums places – reconstructions, genuine ancient sites, etc. – where people re-enact the way people from the past used to live and dress

magnetometer a machine used by geophysicists to measure variations in the Earth's magnetic field, in order to detect buildings and objects beneath the soil

open excavation a dig where the site is simply excavated and remains uncovered (as opposed to *grid* and trench *excavations*)

photogrammetry the science of measuring from photographs to create maps, plans etc.

post hole a hole which once contained a post (or wooden pillar) usually completely rotted away

radiocarbon dating a dating method based on the decay of carbon isotopes (see page 72 for a detailed explanation)

rescue dig an excavation planned to take place before a development is built over it

resistivity survey locating buried buildings and objects using a resistivity meter (See *geophysics*)

ritual connected to some religious or magic practice. (If no obvious function can be given to a site or artefact, the suggestion is often that it's ritual!)

salting secretly planting fakes or finds from elsewhere in an archaeological site, either to give salted artefact *provenance*, or to give misleading information about the site. Often illegal

salvage excavation an emergency dig to salvage what information and artefacts possible before the site is destroyed by, for example, new building

sherds pieces of broken pottery, sometimes called 'potsherds'

sieving, dry when soil is shaken through various sieves to leave behind objects (pebbles, small archaeological finds) for examination

sieving, wet when sediments are mixed with water and poured through sieves. Larger objects (stones, etc.) are caught in the larger-meshed sieve, whilst small organic material (such as pollen, seeds and insects) is washed into a smaller-meshed sieve. (See *flotation*)

spectrometry the identification of minerals and compounds in an artefact by producing a spectrum of light from it. Different spectra reveal the absence or presence of different minerals and compounds

stratigraphy the series of earth deposits, one on top of the other, leaving the oldest at the bottom. Studying a site's stratigraphy is one way of attempting to establish its history

tells mounds created by the constant building on top of previous habitats (normally in regions of building with mud brick)

thermoluminescence dating a dating method based on the measurement of the amount of energy released from a fired clay object, usually pottery (see page 74 for a more detailed explanation)

topography the study of the landscape, both natural and human-made

typology the dating of objects by their variations in style, pattern and function over time

test trench a trench dug to see what it will reveal. Does it match geophysical evidence? Does it pinpoint the position of a previous dig? May be recorded and closed down if not immediately useful

Index